by Anna Jordan

Freak was first produced by Theatre503 and Polly Ingham Productions
at the Edinburgh Festival Fringe in August 2014
and at Theatre503 in September 2014

by Anna Jordan

CAST

Georgie	Lia Burge
Leah	April Hughes

CREATIVE TEAM

Director	Anna Jordan
Lighting Designer	Rachel Bottomley
Designer	Petra Hjortsberg
Stage Manager	Dan Jones

CAST

LIA BURGE (Georgie)
Lia trained at LAMDA. Theatre includes development performances of *Freak* at Theatre503; *Separate Tables* and *The Circle* for Chichester Festival Theatre; *Collaboration/Taking Sides* in the West End; *The Maternal Instinct*, *The Silents* and *The Empire Builders* on the fringe and *Comedy of Errors*, *Romeo and Juliet*, *Macbeth*, *Henry IV Part 1*, *As You Like It* and *Julius Caesar* with The Merely Players rep company at The Cockpit Theatre. Lia has also danced at Glyndebourne and Grange Park Opera and is artistic director of Shakespeare audio-play company BardBox.

APRIL HUGHES (Leah)
April Hughes graduated from E15 drama school in 2012. Her stage work since includes Theatre503 and Soho Theatre in London. Screen work includes the American TV Series *Obsession* and a number of roles for CBBC. The development run of *Freak* was April's first theatre role after graduating and she's thrilled to take it back to the stage.

CREATIVE TEAM

ANNA JORDAN (Writer and Director)
Anna's play *Yen* won the Bruntwood Prize for Playwriting and has a full production at the Royal Exchange Theatre, Manchester, next year. She directed *Tomorrow I'll Be Happy* by Jonathan Harvey at the National Theatre Shed as part of the 2013 Connections Festival. Other awards include Best Play and Audience Award for *Closer To God* (Offcut Festival) and Best New Writing for *Just For Fun – Totally Random* (Lost One Act Festival). Writing/directing credits include *Stay Happy Keep Smiling* (Soho); *BENDER* (Old Red Lion); *Coming Home* (Bush); *Staunch* (Arcola); *Fragments* (Riverside). Writing credits include *Chicken Shop* (Park, September 2014); *The Freedom Light* (Company of Angels); *The Ivory Year* (LAMDA). Directing credits include *Crystal Springs* (Eureka, San Francisco); *Vote of No Confidence, Only Human* (Theatre503). Anna has just finished working on LAMDA's prestigious New Writing Project. She is Artistic Director of *Without a Paddle Theatre,* and teaches acting and playwriting.

RACHEL BOTTOMLEY (Lighting Designer)
Rachel graduated in 2012 from The Liverpool Institute of Performing Arts. In 2012 Rachel was awarded the Association of Lighting Designers Michael Northern Bursary for lighting design for her designs of *A Clockwork Orange* (LIPA) and *The Last Eden* (Dirt Contained). Rachel's other work at Theatre503 includes Lighting Associate for Jo Town on *Life of Stuff* and Lighting Design for *Thatcherwrite* and the recent production of *It Never Ends.*

PETRA HJORTSBERG (Designer)
Petra is a Theatre and Performance Designer who works internationally across a wide range of genres.

Theatre design credits include the OFFIE-nominated *Occupied* (Theatre503); *Companion Piece* (Pleasance, London); *Body Electric* (Best Production and Best Off-Site nominee) & *DISCOnnected* (ABSOLUT Fringe Festival, Dublin); *Treasure this?* as part of *Bush Bazaar* (Bush) and *In Extremis* (King's Head). Costume credits include *Cnoic Chlaonta, Shift(h)er* (USA & Ireland); *Celebrity* (Project Arts Centre, Dublin); *Romeo and Juliet, A Man for All Seasons* (St Paul's School, London); Film and video credits include *Magpie, Way of the Monkey's Claw, The 95th, PubMonkey, Blind Man's Dream, Termination* (UK) as well as costume work for artist Mila Falls and Cloud Boat (UK). In 2013 she was a finalist at the *World Stage Design Exhibition* as well as chosen for participation in *NEXT STAGE* at the Dublin Theatre Festival.

DAN JONES (Stage Manager)
Dan graduated with a degree in Theatre Design and Production in 2003 from Trinity College, Carmarthen. Since then he has worked in a variety of roles including Lighting Designer, Production and Stage Manager. He is currently a resident technician at the Bloomsbury Theatre. Recent credits include *Hope Light and Nowhere* for Suba Das at Underbelly Cowgate; *Women of Troy* at the Bloomsbury Theatre; *The Winter's Tale* a site-specific piece for Suba Das and Old Vic Tunnels; *The Malcontent* for Rae McKen at the White Bear and *Othello* at The Rose on Bankside. Dan worked with Anna Jordan on the development performances of *Freak* at Theatre503 in 2013 and is looking forward to taking the show to the Edinburgh Festival.

POLLY INGHAM
PRODUCTIONS

POLLY INGHAM PRODUCTIONS

Polly Ingham is a freelance theatre producer who specialises in developing new work, both in theatre and musical theatre. She established Polly Ingham Productions in 2012.

Polly is currently Producer and Head of Marketing for Theatre503 working on, among other projects, their two 2014 West End Transfers of *A Handful of Stars*, starring Keith Duffy, and *Land of Our Fathers* by Chris Urch. She is a member of the Clore Emerging Leader Alumni and the Stage One Producer's Workshop.

From September 2012 to September 2013 Polly Ingham was Resident Producer at Oxford Playhouse and Magdalen College School making work for both organisations and collaborating with Resident Director Rosy Banham. She produced three new shows for MCS, a fourth as Polly Ingham Productions, *England Street* by Kenneth Emson in association with Oxford Playhouse and worked on *Where's Father Christmas?*, directed by Helen Eastman, for the Oxford Playhouse. She also line-produced a new adaptation of Golding's *Lord of the Flies* directed by Adrian Noble and Joanne Pearce.

In the same year for Polly Ingham Productions she produced *Dirty Great Love Story* written by Richard Marsh and Katie Bonna. The show enjoyed performances at Bristol Old Vic and the Theatre Royal Bury St Edmunds. Polly previously produced the show with Richard and Katie at the Edinburgh Fringe Festival in August 2012 in the Pleasance Jack Dome, during which the show received a Scotsman Fringe First Award. The show was produced by Polly Ingham Productions and Tim Johanson Productions in association with the Theatre Royal Bury St Edmunds in New York this June at the Brits off Broadway 59E59 Theatre in New York. *Dirty Great Love Story* was also published by Methuen Drama.

Polly also runs Three Pin Productions with West End leading lady Ruthie Henshall and musical director Paul Schofield. To learn more about the company and their work please visit the company page or www.threepinproductions.com.

Prior to her residency in Oxford, Polly produced for Theatre Royal Bury St Edmunds and York Theatre Royal. She is also a member of the Old Vic New Voices club having taken part in the 24 Hour Plays and Ignite 6 in autumn 2011.

Her theatre credits include *A Handful of Stars* (Theatre503/Trafalgar Studios for Theatre503); *Dirty Great Love Story* (59E59Theatres, New York); *England Street* (Burton Taylor Studio, Oxford Playhouse); *Dirty Great Love Story* (Soho/Bristol Old Vic/Theatre Royal Bury St Edmunds); *An Intimate Evening with Ruthie Henshall* (national tour 2013 and 2014); *Where's Father Christmas?* (on behalf of Oxford Playhouse); *Dirty Great Love Story* (Pleasance, Edinburgh); *Shakespeare in the Streets* (Bury Festival); *Backstage Past* (Theatre Royal Bury St Edmunds/National Trust), *Stagefright* (TRBSE); *Time Warner Ignite: Old Vic New Voices* (Old Vic Tunnels); *Dick Whittington and His Cat* (TRBSE); *The 24 Hour Plays: Old Vic New Voices* (Old Vic); *Dick Turpin's Last Ride* (TRBSE/national tour); *Line* (41 Monkgate, York and Stephen Joseph Theatre); *4.48 Psychosis* (York Theatre Royal); *TakeOver Festival* (York Theatre Royal).

THEATRE 503

Theatre503 is the award-winning home of groundbreaking plays.

Led by Artistic Director Paul Robinson, Theatre503 is a flagship fringe venue committed to producing new work that is game-changing, relevant, surprising, mischievous, visually thrilling and theatrical. Our theatre is one of London's few destinations for new writing and we offer more opportunities to new writers than any theatre in the country.

THEATRE503 TEAM

Shine a light on Theatre503.....

Theatre503 receives no public subsidy as a venue and we cannot survive without the transformative support of our friends. For as little as £23 a year you can help us remain 'Arguably the most important theatre in Britain today'

(*Guardian*)

Becoming a Friend of Theatre503 is simple.
Annual Support donations are invited in five tiers:

FOOTLIGHT (£23)
Priority notice of productions and events
Priority booking for all productions
Special ticket offers
E-mail bulletins

SPOTLIGHT (£53)
As Footlight plus
Access to sold-out shows
Credit in the theatre foyer, playtexts, and on the website

LIMELIGHT (£173)
As Spotlight plus
Two complimentary tickets to Theatre503's hottest new play each year
Complimentary tickets to play readings and other one-off supporter events
Free programmes
Ticket exchange service for pre-booked tickets (with 24 hours' notice)

HIGHLIGHT (£503)
As Limelight plus
Two complimentary tickets for each Theatre503 in-house production
Opportunities to attend rehearsals
Invitation to annual high-level supporters' party hosted by the Artistic Director

STARLIGHT (£1003)
A bespoke package enables our Starlight to engage with Theatre503's work as they wish. This can include bespoke entertaining opportunities at the theatre, invitations to attend supper parties with the Artistic Director, or closer engagement with playwrights and the artistic team. Starlights can also choose a strand of Theatre503's work to support, for example a particular production, funding Theatre503 writing programmes or work in the local community. Please visit our website theatre503.com for details on specific appeals also.

One-off donations also make an enormous difference to the way Theatre503 is able to operate. Whether you are able to give £10 or £1000 your gift will help us continue to create work of award-winning standard.

To become a member or make a one-off donation email your interest to: **info@theatre503.com**, or by post to: Theatre503, The Latchmere, 503 Battersea Park Road, London, SW11 3BW.

Alternatively visit our website **theatre503.com** or ring 020 7978 7040 to sign up for membership directly.

If you are a UK tax payer and able to make a gift aid donation please let us know as we receive 25p per pound more on top of your donation in government grant.

FREAK

Anna Jordan

Characters

LEAH, *fifteen*
GEORGIE, *thirty*

This text went to press before the end of rehearsals and so may differ slightly from the play as performed.

One double bed – centre stage. To the left of the bed some make-up, hair products, a cuddly toy or two, a poster image of a generic female pop star – all tits and lips; LEAH's *bedroom. To the right there are clothes strewn, a couple of empty wine bottles, some dirty knickers. Also a few dusty relics from a trip afar to find oneself; beads, a Buddha. Neutral hues. Non-descript Ikea chic, but a bit of a fucking mess;* GEORGIE's *bedroom.*

Both girls use the bed. There is a chair to each side of the bed. In the downstage corner of each room an imagined full-length mirror which the girls use frequently. On the fourth wall each girl has an imagined window. LEAH *stands up on the bed wearing pyjamas and clutching a cuddly toy.* GEORGIE *lies sleeping next to her wearing a large oversized man's shirt.* LEAH *delivers song lyrics in a bright and honest manner, without a hint of cynicism or sexiness.*

Georgie dreams

LEAH *recites the chorus and then the last verse from 'Freak' by Estelle. From 'He wanna see you get down low' she crouches, animalistic, taking on an altogether darker note; building in rhythm.* GEORGIE *tosses and turns a little.* LEAH *ends on:*

LEAH. I can be a – I can be a –

> GEORGIE *sits bolt upright in bed with a gasp as* LEAH *lies back in bed asleep.*
>
> *Beat.* GEORGIE *is breathless.*

GEORGIE. This fucking *dream*!

> I'm raised up on the Fourth Plinth at Trafalgar Square. I've got gaffer tape here and here – (*Indicates her breasts and*

crotch.) and I'm wearing skyscraper heels. I'm dancing, winding; writhing. And the whole of Trafalgar Square is mesmerised by me. Businessmen, tourists, fucking... pigeons. I don't know where the music is coming from but it reverberates in my gut and the lumbar region of my spine. Businessmen are loosening their ties, their shirts are wet with sweat. Japanese men take pictures of me with their Japanese cameras whilst being scolded by their crowfooted dry-cunted Japanese wives.

And every man is hard for me. I mean every man in Trafalgar fucking Square. Fuck it – cocks *all over the* city are filling with blood for me. Denim straining, nylon stretching, buttons popping, zips busting. Stag parties roar and leer at me. Grab their crotches, spit beer at me. All over the city, grooms-to-be are changing their minds because of *me*.

Suddenly there's helicopters. Flashlights. Sirens. It's like a scene from an action movie about the end of the world. We're in America now. The Big Apple now. I'm on top of the Empire State Building. I'm the woman in *King Kong*! (The original – not the remake.) I'm tiny, perhaps the tiniest woman ever made, with fingernails the size of grains of rice. Bones like little twigs, hair like strands of gold. My dress is torn; part of my breast is exposed. He squeezes me, King Kong, his hairy hands impossibly big – his thumb the size of my face. He breathes hot wet gorilla breath which smells of blood and meat and drenches my body. He squeezes me again and laughs, and I think I will piss myself. No one watches now. It's just me and Kong. I know the end of the world is coming but before it comes he's going to take me. Break me. Tear me. End me. I panic. I scream! I wake up. I'm coming.

Long pause.

I reach for him. Instinctively, I reach for James. Then I remember he's gone and I wonder when I'll stop doing this.

Then I remember the bottle and a half of shit rosé wine.

I remember the seven Marlboro Lights I promised not to smoke. (Promised no one but myself.)

I remember swigging and smoking and leaning out of the window and the Turkish men in the shop opposite laughing at me.

I think about hurting myself and laugh at the amount of time I spend thinking about hurting myself and the fact that I never do anything about it because I'm a coward.

I think about my mother and sister's disgust.

I think about cocaine and car crashes and forest fires.

I think about James.

James. Jamie James.

I wonder if he's dreaming.

Beat.

I feel wasted. Not wasted fucked, but wasted unused. Celibate. Wretched. I feel a profound sense of displacement; of wasted dreams and missed opportunities. My body is wet. My youth soaked into the sheets. I try to make myself cum again but I can't and it makes me angry. I feel like a child having a tantrum.

I try to vomit. I can't vomit. I watch the clock. I drink tea. I watch the clock. I marvel at the length of a minute. I watch a minute become an hour and I gawp at the length of an hour. I think of the desolation and cold-calling tomorrow has to offer.

I watch shit shit television. *Super Casino*, repeats of *Countdown*. I long to be sucked into the screen and for my body to fragment into a million pixels. American football, Babestation, *Danny Dyer's Deadliest Men*.

I lose myself. Finally.

Every fucking night.

She lies back down and tries to sleep.

Leah plucks

LEAH *is sitting up on the end of the bed, plucking hairs out of her arm with tweezers.*

LEAH. There's an average of five million hairs on the human body. If it takes me two point five seconds to pluck out one hair, it's gonna take me three thousand four hundred and seventy-two hours twenty-two minutes to pluck my entire body smooth, like an eel. I didn't just work that out in my head. I'm not some Curious-Dog-In-The-Night-Time child. It's just I was bored off my tits in Citizenship so I worked it out.

Leanne Beasley worked all summer at Thorpe Park and saved up the money to get her fanny lasered. She said she could smell the hairs burning, and it smelt like bacon and death. Her mum went schiz, kept saying 'What if you change your mind? What if you change your mind?' and Leanne was like 'When am I ever gonna want pubes?' Her mum sold the Wii on Ebay as a punishment but Leanne's never home to play it. She spends all her time round Ashden Fraser's house with her bare naked minge on display. She says he grins at it.

Beat. She looks down.

I didn't know what to do with mine. I asked Sophie about it, she's my best friend, but she went all red and I think secretly she just lets hers *grow*. PUKE. Leanne said that shaving it was 'a road I did *not* want to go down', and that once her cousin got hers waxed and they nearly pulled a lip off. So I bought some Veet, from Superdrug. It smells sickly-sweet like gone-off air freshener, and you have to put it like everywhere to make sure you get like all of them – otherwise Leanne says you end up with an arsehole mullet!

The first time I Veeted it felt so strange. So papery and thin I thought I'd never want anyone to touch it. Ever. But for the past week I've been Veeting *every night*. It gets a bit sore, and it's costing me a fortune but sometimes at break I meet Luke at the back of the DT block and he puts his hand up my skirt and I think 'What about the hair? What if he touches the hair?'

Luke! How can I describe him? Six foot one, sandy hair, green eyes, tight chest. Eyelashes unfairly long for a boy. The fittest most popular boy in year eleven. And he chose ME. Little old Leah. Pretty but geeky. And honestly, the last four weeks have been a whirlwind! Now every day it's me, Leanne, Ashden and Luke – like a famous foursome. Sophie feels left out, but one day she'll understand.

Every Saturday Mum, Dad and Alex do this crappy car boot, selling our old toys and junk for the holiday fund to Kefalonia. (I am *definitely* not going.) So Luke comes here. To *my* bedroom. And every week it's something new. At first he would kiss me hard and lay on top of me so all the air went out of me, and that was the first time I felt something happening, a burning in my stomach and a sort of lightness in my legs and a fluttering in my chest. And I guess that's what being *turned on* feels like. It feels like something you need to fix. And it feels like anything could happen.

The next week I felt his dick hard against my leg and I laughed. He didn't like it. But I couldn't believe it felt like that; it just seemed like such a… cliché. But then I felt myself getting wet between my legs and that felt very grown up. He started to rub himself against me, like we were having sex but with our clothes on. In PSHE Miss Pringle said that was called *frottage*, and Leanne said she thought that was a type of cheese and I laughed Sprite out of my nostrils.

The next time he asked to touch my tits. I had to let him, but I felt self-conscious because they're not big and round like Sophie's or hard and perky like Leanne's. But it was okay. Then he kissed them. And that was okay. But *then* he started sucking them, which I found utterly disgusting because I kept picturing him as a big baby in a nappy and I had to run to the loo.

When I came back he'd got it out. His dick. I'd never seen one like that… all hard like that. Not in the flesh. Suddenly the Snapchat he'd sent of it seemed… safe. I wanted to stare at it for ages but I wanted to look away too. He took my hand and put it around the… base. I gave it a squeeze and it sort of flinched. I got flustered and told him that was enough for today, and he laughed. After he left I wanted to tell someone about it. I thought about texting Sophie but she wouldn't understand. I thought about texting Leanne, but she's seen loads of dicks. So I just texted Luke, saying how hot I thought it was, seeing his cock all hard like that, and he texted straight back saying I WANT TO PUT IT INSIDE YOU.

I put my phone down. And I lay on my bed. (*Lies down on the bed*.) And I put my hand here. (*Puts her hand on her crotch*.) And I wondered how much longer this will just be mine.

LEAH *falls asleep*.

Georgie's epiphany

GEORGIE *stands up on the bed in her shirt. She recites the chorus and first verse of 'Dirty Talk' by Wynter Gordon. The lyrics are delivered in a slightly monotonous yet rhythmic way.* LEAH *sits straight up in bed and joins in halfway through the first verse, ending on:*

GEORGIE/LEAH. Cherry pop, tag team, can you make me –

LEAH *gets up with a jolt and a gasp as though awaking from a dream and gets off the bed to sit in her chair.* GEORGIE *plonks herself down on the end of the bed. She is energetic, bright.*

GEORGIE. Have you ever woken up and there's an idea just there, right there hanging above your face and you reach out and you just fucking grab it. And it's not God talking to you, or Allah or Buddha or your pet fucking dead dog or anything like that. It's life. Communicating with you straight down the fucking line.

I take a picture of myself doing this – (*Holds her middle finger up to the phone and takes a picture*.) and send it

straight to Kerry-Ann at the agency with the message
'LATERS MOTHERFUCKERS'.

FUCK! No more Kerry-Ann. Ah, Kerry-Ann with her self-tan
shit streaks and her crooked teeth and the putrid waft of
Femfresh emanating from her crotch every time she moves a
millimetre. No more timesheets, no more cold-calls, no more
staring into the shredder wondering what happened to my life.

The day starts brilliantly. I smoke fags out of the window, try
on every piece of clothing I own and see how many times I
can cum during *Homes Under the Hammer*. I lie with my
head hanging off the bed and listen to the breeze and the cars
and the birds. And I wonder how long I can do this? Opt out
of the real world and fester in my lair, living on cheese and
crisp sandwiches. Nobody knows where I am any more.
Nobody knows now Jamie's gone.

Loneliness closes its grip around my windpipe and so I
switch on *This Morning*. There's a man with a tumour the
size of a tennis ball in his neck and it makes me think of
Dad. At the hospice. And his funeral. Where Mum and
Laura charge ahead into the church. I end up stuck between
our next-door neighbours Mr and Mrs Bartlett, who squeeze
my hand and breathe their boozy breath on me all
throughout the service.

My sister leaves me another voicemail. Sickly simpering.
'Georgina. Georgina.' Fucking *Georgina*. I delete the
voicemails and then Laura's number and my mother's
number too. I feel alone but liberated. I venture out into the
world. And that's when The Fear sets in.

Beat.

Sitting in the corner of a Slug and Lettuce at 2.49 p.m., I
drain a bottle of balsamic Chardonnay and wonder what the
fuck I'm going to do. You know the only two things I've
ever been good at were fucking and football? Genuinely. My
dad would take me to Cleetnorth Park to play, early every
Saturday when the rest of the world was asleep. When we
got home Mum and Laura would be at ballet and we'd eat all

the things that were out of bounds. Crisps. Coke. Nutella. I was his boy. I stopped playing after he died.

Still went to Cleetnorth though, with the lads. Squeeze a tit for a finger of Twix. Hand jobs for a Lambert. Suck it for a Strongbow.

I lean back into the sofa and hope the plump faux leather will swallow me up. I close my eyes and for a moment I feel the dream bass throb through my body and the gaffer tape against my nipples.

'You cannot sleep here.' Bitch barmaid wakes me from my dubstep slumber. I shuffle along the high street, the sun which heartened me taunts me now. I feel fucking fucking low. I plan to head to the nearest chemist, then pop two one-a-night Nytols and sleep till next week. And then I see it. It's new. Almost hidden round the back of Marks and Spencers. CHERRY LOUNGE GENTLEMAN'S CLUB. 'Looking for dancers.'

At home, armed with more shit wine and a delirious air of mischief, I start my application process. Their website asks me if I 'look hot and sexy' and if I'm 'outgoing and friendly' which makes me laugh as my idea of hell is other people. Age: I tell them I'm twenty-five. Thirty is no good for Cherry Lounge. Just past the peak. Starting to sour. Twenty-four hours later I receive my 'audition slot'.

I wait in the bar with a gaggle of skinny plastic girls. My audition is in the VIP lounge with a large cheap-suited man and forty-something fake-titted Scouser. They ask about my dance experience. I tell them about the lost weekends raving on podiums at Bagleys and Turnmills but they look at me blankly and I feel like a cunt. Then it's time. And at 3 p.m. on a rainy Wednesday I peel off my bra to the strains of the Pussycat Dolls. It's hard. I imagine Mother's face, cold and unforgiving, Jamie's face – but with Dad's twinkle, my cat, Boris Johnson, lounging on the window sill, laughing at me.

But then the bass drops and something happens. My body is flooded with energy, and the music seeps through me, and

I'm no longer a thirty-year-old jobless friendless sadsack cunt, I'm on the Fourth Plinth with the gaffer tape and the hard dicks all over the city. And I get the fucking job. I get the fucking job. And tomorrow I will take my clothes off for a living.

GEORGIE *laughs and falls back on the bed, arms open.*

Leah's naked experience

LEAH *sits on the bed in her pyjamas and pulls her knees to her.*

LEAH. The first time I saw a naked woman I was five. Mum took me swimming. I came out of the cubicle we were changing in I got the shock of my life. These two women, proper old, at least forty, were walking around like totally stark-fucking-naked. One was all bony and thin, with sagging skin on her stomach and these tiny tits, like deflated balloons. And the other had this enormous drooping belly and massive tits like pendulums swinging. And they both had these enormous fucking hairy bushes between their legs. They strutted, chatted, rubbed cream in themselves, like it was the most natural thing in the world. I cried. They laughed. Mum smacked me. It was awful.

Every morning I get up before everyone else and run four miles. I've started the 5:2 diet but I do more like 3:4 or 4:3 because it's really not that hard to survive on five hundred calories a day. Mum doesn't know. Sometimes I only eat dinner. But I'm happy like this. I like it like this.

Over the following text GEORGIE *gets ready to go out. She applies make-up. She takes off her oversized shirt, underneath is a basque which might form part of a lap dancer's outfit, and little shorts. She does not need to stay just in this for any length of time as she puts on a large black winter coat which has a belt in preparation for going out.*

GEORGIE. I now exist in an exclusive nocturnal parallel universe. I snooze all day and watch porn and ignore my sister's phone calls. I eat instant noodles and drink tea and vodka and wait for the dark. I clean my body, shave my body and apply war paint. I put on my warm winter coat and hail down a black cab.

The club booms with cheap dirty beats. Synthetic. Urgent. Haunting. The other girls are vacuous and foreign but I share lines of coke and lip gloss with them in the dressing rooms. The heat of aroused men burns through the air-con chill. They think I am the most beautiful thing in the world. And I don't mind being a thing. I don't want their respect I want only their animal desire. Wide boys, rude boys, wise guys, city types. Payday punters; the skin-headed boy-men with sad eyes and stubble, smelling like Joop and B&H, all Stella and brandy and weekends and madness. Young professionals in their Armani suits, with their rich pissed clients and their too-loud voices. Quiet, indistinct men who drink alone.

During LEAH's *following text* GEORGIE *racks up a line of coke.*

LEAH. This evening Mum, Dad and Alex had pizza and a DVD and I locked myself away up here. I watch Rihanna videos. Rihanna is so sexy and I am so lucky because I don't know how to be sexy but Rihanna can show me. I google porn and watch women dressed like school girls, women kissing women, women opening themselves up like I never thought… I watch oral, anal and other things that make me shaky. Then I take off all my clothes and study every inch of myself in the mirror. Get into every position I might find myself in with him; legs open, arching my back, on all-fours, touching my toes. I take photos. Think about sending them to Luke. Delete them. I record myself. I practise what I might look like when I cum for the first time. I use the camera to look at my… (*Indicates between her legs.*) I mean *really* look. (*Beat.*) The human body is a strange strange fucking strange thing.

I lay in bed with no clothes on. And I feel like I'm a very small person in a very big bed in a huge house in a massive world just playing at being grown up. I can sense them downstairs, on the sofa, Alex in the middle; warm. There's a sort of glow to them. I want to put on my jammies and join; throw popcorn at Alex and put my feet on Dad's lap like always, but I can't. I'm trapped here, naked, in no man's land. The things I've looked at and the things I've done make me ashamed and excited at the same time. My whole body throbs and aches. I wonder if the only way to get rid of it is to touch myself and so I do, I try it, but it just feels like nothing so I put on my jammies and brush my teeth three times. Then I go to sleep, and dream I'm up on Dad's shoulders at the fair or I'm playing out with Sophie with our favourite dolls and teddies.

GEORGIE. I dance for them. (*Snorts a line of coke.*) I strip. And every face, every expression coaxes me to go further, get lower, open wider, do more. And when I'm totally bare their eyes cover me, clothe me. It's like a new kind of naked. They like it when I bite my finger and look confused and innocent. And they like it when I look sort of afraid.

But I am not afraid. I am formidable. All meat all sex all vulnerable all powerful. I'm in on a secret; part of a club. And all of my failings – all of them. My stubborn cuntedness. My inability to show love or be loved. My hatred of babies. My messiness. My sluttiness. The fact that I didn't see Dad – at the end. All washed away by one simple act: the sharing of my body with the men in this room. I feel worshipped. Forgiven. I am theirs. She-God-Little-Girl-Lioness.

Music. LEAH *and* GEORGIE *look in their mirrors.*
GEORGIE *peels off her coat to the music and discards it.*
LEAH *undresses nervously in front of the mirror to girly knickers and vest – the opposite of* GEORGIE's *underwear. There is a sense of ritual about both of their actions. Then* LEAH *scatters tissues and a few items of clothing around the floor.* GEORGIE *messes her hair using water and drags her make-up down her face. Both sit gingerly on the side of the bed. The following text almost overlaps.*

Music snaps off – lights flick up to a stark light.

The event

LEAH. Luke's just left.

GEORGIE. I've done something bad.

> GEORGIE *throws the duvet over her head and hides.*

LEAH. I don't know why I feel like crying. It's not that I didn't... I mean it wasn't... It's hard to put a word to it... Because it really really was beautiful. Really.

> GEORGIE *comes out from under the duvet a little.*

GEORGIE. Bad bad. Very bad.

> LEAH *starts getting dressed into her pyjamas.*

LEAH. It hurt a bit. Leanne said it definitely wouldn't, because I've used Super Tampax before, but it did.

> GEORGIE *recites the first three lines of 'Dirty Talk' by Wynter Gordon, like a mantra. She puts her head back under the covers.*

He arrives. He looks different. Hair neat and combed, face sweaty and flushed. He tastes like Listerine, smells like pine.

GEORGIE (*emerging, talking fast, panicked*). I'm dreading the end of the night. Thinking about back here, just me and Boris Johnson, the coke wearing off and being alone with my thoughts. Guys start to drift. Girls order taxis, text their boyfriends. But I've got a half of a gram left and I'm flying on the thrill of the night.

> GEORGIE *gets into her oversized shirt, feeling exposed.*

There's a group of stags in the VIP, I've given one of them a private dance earlier. They're still going strong, buzzing off cheap champagne and charlie, flashing the cash, bouncing off the walls. So I think maybe I'll just join them for a drink. Yeah. Maybe. One. Drink.

LEAH. We hold hands, walk upstairs.

GEORGIE. We down jägers, chat shit.

LEAH. He trips up on the way into my room. I catch him and we laugh. He's nervous.

GEORGIE. Billy, Aaron, Dev. Gareth? The stag's called George, like me. They're fit. Young. Sharp clothes. White teeth. Sure of themselves. Trusting of their cocks. They pour drink after drink. They tell me I'm fit. They drink to that. They drink to me.

LEAH. He turns the TV on and stands near it changing the channel again and again. I stand next to him and watch the programmes flash by. I take his hand.

GEORGIE. We leave the club.

LEAH. I give it a squeeze. It's wet in the palm.

GEORGIE. The back of a taxi. Me in the middle, warm.

LEAH. I intertwine my fingers with his.

GEORGIE. One kisses my neck. One squeezes my tits.

LEAH. I pull him to me so we're shoulder to shoulder.

GEORGIE. They both put their hands inside of my coat.

LEAH. I squeeze it again. I look into his eyes.

GEORGIE. One grabs my crotch. Their mate takes a photo.

LEAH. I think this is real!

GEORGIE. I pretend I've been kidnapped.

LEAH. He turns off the TV.

GEORGIE. We pull up at a house.

Beat.

Under his breath the cabbie says, 'I'm glad you're not my daughter.' They roar at him. A barrage of expletives. One kicks his cab. My protectors. My knights in shining armour.

LEAH. We sit on the bed. I take off my top. He unbuttons his shirt. We're laughing. The two of us. Laughing, on the edge of the bed.

GEORGIE. The house is slick and modern. Leather/chrome. Shagpad/showhome. I go to the toilet, I rack up my coke in one fat line and snort it off the loo seat. I look in the mirror for about one minute. Then that luscious chemical hit takes over and I'm ready for anything. I reapply my lipstick and stride into the lounge.

LEAH. He kisses me and moves his tongue deep in my mouth. I think about asking him to use it down there, just to know how it feels, but I know that he won't.

GEORGIE. They're waiting for me. Mischievous. Expectant.

LEAH. He helps me undress, his hands damp and shaky.

GEORGIE. The boys lose their watches, phones go off, blinds come down. We stave off the morning. We drown out the birds. We cheat time.

LEAH. We're both in our pants now.

GEORGIE. We laugh. We down shots. We snort. We smoke.

LEAH. We kiss and tangle ourselves in the bed sheets.

GEORGIE. I match them drink for drink, line for line. Sit on laps, tell dirty jokes, hold court. They pass me around like a doll, like a trophy. I'm the best thing since sliced bread. Wearing my game face. Up-for-it-fucked-up-sexy-bitch.

LEAH. He peels off my knickers and there I am. Naked. For the first time with somebody else since Alex and I shared a bath. I look down and I'm pleased with what I see. Pleased I look neat and bare.

GEORGIE. Proper rushing now. The bass of the dubstep throbs through the speakers. I'm more than turned on; I feel a deep sense of thrill, foreboding, lust. A profound connection to the moment, like I'm properly committed to something for the very first time. I adore these men. I adore these five men. And I'm going to show them just how I adore them.

LEAH. I press my tits against his chest and the warmth of it just feels amazing and I wonder if we could just do this for a bit.

GEORGIE. I dance for them. An exclusive VIP show. They cheer and applaud and get hard in their pants. I let them undress me, pull at me, stroke me. I tell them 'No touching rule doesn't apply'. They exchange glances, shrugs, winks, nods. I know what they're thinking. They're thinking...

LEAH. He puts his fingers inside me for the first time.

GEORGIE. They're thinking...

LEAH. Properly. In me.

GEORGIE. They're thinking FUCK IT. Let's Do This.

LEAH. And the *significance* of it, putting part of *his* body *inside my* body, meant more than the way it actually felt which was a bit funny and a bit sore. I thought it would feel more...

GEORGIE. I'm down on my knees.

LEAH.... When something was *inside* me.

GEORGIE. Hands go to flies, zips unzipped and buttons popped. Their faces. As eager and horny as the boys in Cleetnorth Park. Men, boys, all the same, I love them for being ruled by their cocks.

LEAH. He gently pushes on my shoulders and suddenly I'm face to face with his dick.

GEORGIE. The stag gets the first go. He gets his cock out.

LEAH. I take a deep breath.

GEORGIE. And I go to work.

Both take a breath.

LEAH. It tastes like soap and it's hot and I understand why they call it a boner. It's like the weirdest thing ever. I try to fit it all in my mouth, he makes this gasping noise and grabs the back of my head and I gag. I think he likes that.

GEORGIE. His cock is in my mouth, and the others get theirs out, wank themselves, surround me. It's like a textbook porno and I'm the star. I stare up at them with these big baby-doll eyes that say, 'Oh *my*, you're so *big*, you're not going to hurt me are you?' I take turns, two at a time. They moan and gasp and goad me and tease me. *I* am responsible for *all* this pleasure. I stick cocks down my throat and make my eyes water.

LEAH. He pulls me up to him, his eyes kind of wild. He lays me down, supporting my neck and head in this old-fashioned gesture. He strokes my face and I think he's going to tell me that he loves me. But he tells me that I'm beautiful. Which is pretty much the same thing, right? Then he jumps up, off the bed. He's gone.

GEORGIE. Gag. Spit.

LEAH. Where? Why?

GEORGIE. Choke. Retch.

LEAH. 'Stop,' I say. He just smiles and picks up his jeans. I feel tears coming. But then he laughs and shushes me and holds up a condom. He tears it open and I have to look away then, as I think he looks a bit stupid bent over his cock trying to get it on. With my face turned away I have a very clear thought.

GEORGIE. No going back now.

LEAH. This is the very last few moments of something. Then he's on top of me.

GEORGIE. I'm on all-fours on the living-room mat. Expensive. Persian. Egyptian. Or something. As I reach out a hand grabs my wrist. It's Gareth, I think? A little older, grey around the sides. He pulls me towards him and says, 'Sweetheart, are you sure about this?' The boys swear and jeer and I laugh. Then I silence his fears with a long French kiss, the kind reserved for boyfriends or husbands only. I tell him I want him to fuck me first.

LEAH. He nudges my legs apart and we fit together, his bony hips graze the inside of my thighs. It's all happening. Faster than I thought it would.

GEORGIE. Gareth kneels behind me. His hands on my arse cheeks.

LEAH. Oh my God there's an inch. Another inch. And he…
He…

GEORGIE. He puts his cock inside me.

LEAH. There it is. Inside me.

Beat.

I'm having sex! I'm making love! I'm fucking! He looks like
a different person. Concentrating very hard. He seems to be
in a place that I can't join him. And for a moment I panic. I
think that maybe I could just slide out from under him and
tiptoe downstairs and watch telly while he thrusts away. But
he stops. He looks at me. He smiles. He kisses me. He gasps.
He kisses me. This is what you'd call… sensual?

GEORGIE. This is what you'd call a spit-roast. George at the
front, Gareth at the back. The rest of them watching,
wanking. It's electric. Then they confer and swap ends. And
George just fucking goes for it. A can't-believe-his-luck
fuck. A Brucie-fuckin-bonus fuck. All the things his
girlfriend won't let him do: grab my tits, slap my arse, pull
my hair right from the roots. The others follow his lead:
Someone holds my nose. There are hands around my throat.
Spit and fingers in my arsehole.

LEAH. He whispers in my ear. Moans 'Leah' and 'Baby'.

GEORGIE. They're saying 'Her 'and 'She'. Like I'm not there.

LEAH. 'You feel so good. You feel amazing.'

GEORGIE. 'Turn her over. Move her here.'

LEAH. 'Leah baby.'

GEORGIE. 'Fucking whore.'

Beat.

They're all at it now. Cocks in every hole. This is what I
wanted. But I thought I would be *involved*. Now my thoughts,
my words, my will; none of them matter because they are
well and truly In Me. And it hurts. I'm scared that something
inside me might break. So I close my eyes and try to focus on

giving myself to them completely. I meditate on how it feels
to be connected to so many people at once. How I could
really forget myself and who I am and all the things I've said
and done and places I've been and thoughts I've had. Like a
Total System Restore. And I go completely fucking vacant.
Just an 'Oh yeah' or a 'Fuck me harder' every few seconds.
No brain engaged just meat and holes. Mouth Pussy Arse
Mouth Pussy Arse. They change places. Crack jokes. Smoke
cigarettes. Tag team. A couple of them cum, on my face and
in my hair and on my back and then sit on the sofa and watch
the others. And then something fucking weird happens. It's
like I leave my body and I'm able to look down on myself.
I'm pale, and skinnier than I've ever been. I'm being pulled
this way and that. We look like animals. The boys are some
sort of wild bears fighting over a young dead deer or
something. A dead fawn. Then I snap back into myself and
I'm making this awful noise. This awful, primal, non-female
noise. There's arguing, shouting, and there's something inside
me. Something cold and hard. Someone shouts 'Get it out'
and someone else shouts 'Calm the fuck down' and they take
whatever it is out and throw it across the room and hear it
smash so I guess it was a bottle or something.

Pause.

LEAH. Passionate. Honest. Gentle. Tender. Might be words I
would use to describe my first time.

GEORGIE. I wait to be filled up again, but they leave me empty.

LEAH. Ridiculous. Strange. Silly. Awful.

GEORGIE. Gaping.

LEAH. Wonderful.

GEORGIE. Cold.

LEAH. Terrifying.

Beat.

Luke cums like a lot lot lot lot lot lot lot lot lot lot lot quicker
than I expected him to.

GEORGIE. The front door slams; Gareth. Footsteps into the kitchen. The last two hang around, half-hearted, but one can't get hard now, the other says 'It's a fucking mess down here' and they drift off. Just lost interest, I guess. Like an abandoned game of Sunday morning five-a-side. I lie still. I hear cans of beer being opened and a kettle boiling. Someone covers me with a throw from the sofa, perhaps to keep me warm, perhaps so he doesn't have to look at me. And I'm alone.

LEAH. I had imagined us in all different positions. All the ways I had wanted him to see me. But he just gives this little shudder and makes this little noise which, thinking about it now, might have actually been the word 'No'. Then he lies very still, on top of me for so long, that I think he might have passed out or died.

GEORGIE. I lay there very still for a long time, hoping that I might pass out or die.

LEAH. He comes to life again. Looks at me: proud. He says, 'Leah, you're so fit', throws the duvet over our heads, and pulls me close. And *now* I am in heaven, with my man. In our little marshmallow world, our grown-up naked bodies wound around each other, legs entangled. I can smell his breath and his sweat and it smells sweet and we begin to drift and dream together and it is *perfect*. When they're in Kefalonia we can do this *every night*.

GEORGIE. As I lie there on the mat I think about my dad. I think about the coat he used to wear. The bag he took to work. His weekend shoes. An old wound begins to open and so I grab fistfuls of the throw that covers me and hold on for dear life. It feels expensive. Like someone took time and energy and care to make it. On a loom. Thousands upon thousands of stitches. I try to count them. I begin to fade. Not into sleep exactly but into a sort of nothingness.

LEAH. We fall asleep.

Long pause.

GEORGIE. I come to. I can smell things. Day-old aftershave. Bacon. Cum. I turn my head and the entire world shudders and spins on its axis. My coat laid neatly on the sofa. Next to it, forty pounds. I steady myself against the wall and inside I howl. I retrieve my clothes, shoes from behind the plant pot, underwear from the cracks in the sofa. I put my coat on and tie the belt tightly around my waist, imagining it is holding me together. I grab the cash and walk to the front door.

In the hall George the stag, my namesake, weeps gently on the stairs.

LEAH. We wake up cos my phone rings. 'MUM.' Do I want something from Starbucks? A hot chocolate or a massive cookie? Hearing her voice is weird. I think she's been crying, problems with my auntie. And I hear Dad in the background, arguing with Alex. I try to sound normal, but I'm a whole new person and they don't even know. Luke is snoring and the condom full of cold spunk is pressing against my back. I wake him and I tell him he needs to go and I nuzzle into his chest but then – and I can't believe this – I start to cry. He thinks it's weird and I pull away because I feel like a dick, but also what I really want is a cuddle from my dad.

GEORGIE. In the taxi my phone pings. Seven messages from Laura. I throw it out of the window because I don't believe I deserve a mobile phone. The cabbie laughs and shakes his head. What an ugly idiotic spastic cunt, he thinks. On the journey I think about George and his Mrs. I think she's called Margaret. Which is stupid because nobody's called Margaret nowadays. I think about him and Margaret having a bottle of Pinot Grigio in front of *X Factor* on a Saturday night. I think of the kisses they share; kisses with years of history and the promise of good loving thorough sex in the not too distant future. I think about how one day he'll plant a little seed inside her and it'll grow into a whole new person who will have thoughts and feelings just like us. And I think about how that seed and that growth and that person will always have a little bit of poison in it. Because of me.

LEAH. Wouldn't the world be a different place if men didn't have to put themselves inside women to have sex?

GEORGIE. Have I got a tumour?

LEAH. And to have sex we had this sort of pair of lips, here, instead of our genitals.

GEORGIE. It feels I've got a tumour.

LEAH. Which kind of suckered together, on the surface.

GEORGIE. It feels like I *am* a tumour.

LEAH. It would be much more equal I think.

GEORGIE. And it's big and growing and it's my whole body and it's cancerous and putrid and if you ripped it open, well then I'm pretty sure the whole of my stinking insides would come rushing out of it. All sorts of blood and guts and horrible thoughts and rotten ideas would spill out onto the floor. And Boris Johnson would lick it a bit but it would taste fucking disgusting, like gone-off liver and cum and vomit. And all that would be left is a sack of dry skin, and brittle bones made of shit cocaine.

LEAH. It's amazing how your world can change in an hour.

GEORGIE. That's what would happen.

LEAH. You can become a new person.

GEORGIE. Tumour. Holes. Blood. Cocaine.

LEAH. I suddenly feel very old.

GEORGIE. I quite like the sound of that.

Each walks to the window on their respective side. LEAH *is looking at her parents arriving home in the car.* GEORGIE *is looking at the Turkish shop across the road.*

I quite like the thought of it.

LEAH. They're back.

Lights snap change. GEORGIE *and* LEAH *make eye contact for the first time.*

(*Quietly.*) Who run the world?

GEORGIE. Girls.

LEAH. Who run the world?

GEORGIE. Girls.

LEAH. Who run the world?

GEORGIE. Girls.

LEAH. Who run the world?

GEORGIE. Girls.

LEAH (*shouting*). Who are we? What do we run?

GEORGIE (*shouting*). The world!

LEAH (*shouting*). Who are we? What do we run?

GEORGIE (*shouting*). The world!

> *Dubstep. Distorted and more aggressive than before.* LEAH
> *takes off her pyjamas and throws them over the bed to*
> GEORGIE. GEORGIE, *in her fucked state, puts them on.*
> LEAH *gets dressed in school uniform, checking herself*
> *frequently in the mirror, giving sass and attitude. They swap*
> *sides.* GEORGIE *clambers into* LEAH*'s bed.* LEAH *sits*
> *gingerly on the end of* GEORGIE*'s bed, and looks around.*
> *During the following text* GEORGIE *should remove her*
> *make-up with a wipe.*

The aftermath

LEAH. Luke can't come to mine because I'm sleeping on the sofa. My Auntie Georgie is staying in my room because she's having a nervous breakdown. Last Saturday she walked into a Turkish supermarket and took her coat off. It turns out she had nothing on underneath. She started shouting, 'Who's gonna fuck me then?' and trying to get the men to touch her and stuff. Then she tripped backwards and fell into a tower of chickpeas and knocked herself out. When they took her to hospital the doctors examined her and they said that there was physical evidence... that she had been raped.

But Auntie Georgie *hasn't* been raped and she *hasn't* been working as a prostitute and she just wants to sleep. That's what she shouted at my mum, anyway. Then my mum tried to put her arm round her and she went fucking nuts and so the doctor came. He gave her some strong sedatives and she's pretty much been sleeping ever since.

That's why I'm here. To feed her spastic cat.

LEAH *has a proper snoop around the flat, there might be some stripper-esque clothes lying around.*

GEORGIE (*reading a copy of* Zoo). The first time I saw a naked woman I was at school. We were doing papier mâché and there were newspapers all over the floor. I remember seeing this young girl, with her bare breasts out looking at the camera sort of all hopeful and chirpy and... lost. It seemed sad, her down there amongst all the rubbish. I've never forgotten it. I wonder why Leah has this.

She puts the magazine down and looks around the room.

LEAH. Boris!

GEORGIE. When Leah was nine or ten we used to be close. She thought I was very cool.

LEAH. Fucking stupid name for a...

GEORGIE. I used to do her make-up.

LEAH. Fucking cat! God she doesn't have anything in this
place it's so… bare.

GEORGIE. And she'd tell me about the boys in her year at
school. List them in order of how cute they were. Laura was
tough on her. She needed some fun.

LEAH. We can't go to Luke's so on Friday we went to Ashden
Fraser's house. I thought I might enjoy it more this time, but
I didn't. Ashden Fraser doesn't wash his sheets and the room
smelt like rank socks covered up with deodorant. Luke went
harder than before, and I could hear Ashden Fraser
downstairs on the X-Box, killing things. He got me to put
my legs up on his shoulders which hurt and made me feel
stupid, all munched up like that, but he *really* loved it. And
he lasted longer this time. Five, maybe six minutes.

GEORGIE (*looking at her walls*). Now posters I had. But Wu-
Tang Clan and Tarantino films. Who are these fucking
women?

LEAH. Afterwards he told me that all the boys in our year were
jealous of him, especially Ashden Fraser! Which made me
feel so fucking good that I forgot all about the jizzy sheets
and the legs on shoulders. Then he got up and got dressed
and went for a piss. He was ages so I put my bra and
knickers on. Then the handle on the door went, but it was
Ashden Fraser with a Goodfellas and a litre of Coke. I
covered myself up but he just looked at me, then he laughed
and sat down and opened his laptop. Luke came back in and
smiled. I pulled my jeans on but Ashden Fraser was sitting
on my top. He threw it to Luke and they played catch with it
for a bit. All the time they were laughing like it was just a
proper joke. So I laughed too and in the end I just sat on the
bed with my arms folded across my chest.

GEORGIE. Jamie came to see me. For a minute I thought it was
my dad, sitting there. He held my hand. He stroked the inside
of my wrist and it felt so beautiful it made me want to
scream. He cried a bit. He was never very tough. I think
there's someone new. He didn't stay long.

LEAH. Then we put some tunes on and ate pizza, like nothing had happened.

GEORGIE. At night now I dream of fingers and fists in holes and flesh being squeezed and twisted. And the resilience of the flesh is lost. It buckles and breaks like parched leather and bleeds black syrup blood. I dream about such violence. But when I wake up I think about James holding my hand. It really soothes me. I know that he's not my boy now and he won't be again but that's okay, you see. Because what gets me through nowadays is this realisation I had when I was not very well at all; that Everything is Transient.

And one day I'll be in my fifties, and I might wear corduroy trousers and have a dog called Pepper and grow things in my garden that need love and attention. Or perhaps I'll be a mummy like Laura, and I'll have teenage daughters like Leah, who despair of me and swear at me under their breath. Or perhaps I'll get cancer and die in my forties and they'll bury me next to my dad. And the roots of the trees and plants will grow deep into the ground and entwine around our bones, and reunite us.

Or maybe I won't.

But what I mean is. It won't be now. And it won't be then. That night. Isn't any more. The sun rises and sets, the tide comes in and goes out. We get older. Things die and change and are born. And die. And one day, I won't exist any more and I take great comfort from that.

LEAH. Luke said he really wanted to think of a present we could give to Ashden to say thank you. He asked me if I had any ideas.

I said maybe an iTunes voucher. Luke laughed and kissed me on my head.

I think he wants me to –

GEORGIE. When I was first here I would slip in and out of sleep and sometimes Laura would be sitting on the end of the bed. And she would talk and talk. And sometimes she'd stroke my hair which felt so alien. I couldn't make out the words. But while she talked I remembered that day in the church when I'd been stuck between our boozy neighbours, she reached her arm past Mrs Bartlett and squeezed the back of my neck, and left her hand there for the whole service.

LEAH. Leanne sucked Luke off while Ashden fucked her in a cupboard on New Year's Eve.

GEORGIE. Laura's done an amazing job with Leah.

LEAH. I know because she told me and she said she didn't regret it.

GEORGIE. She's warm underneath it all. Proper. Loving.

LEAH. It might be really… wild to do two boys together. I mean I'm so flattered, right, the two fittest boys in our year? I can be a freak. I can. Two months ago no one even knew who I was at school and look at me now.

Suddenly LEAH *has an idea. She looks around. She lies back on the pillow and takes a selfie with the keys in her other hand. She sends it to Luke. Then she gets up, bounces on the bed a little, leans down and sniffs the sheet.*

I wonder how many guys my auntie's fucked on this bed.

Beat. She looks around.

This whole place reeks of sex.

She strikes a provocative pose on the end of the bed and looks at herself in GEORGIE*'s mirror.* GEORGIE *turns over into the fetal position.*

Going home

Lights fade. Music. LEAH *crosses round back into her own side.* GEORGIE *is folding clothes.* LEAH *hangs around.*

LEAH. You look like shit.

GEORGIE. Thanks, Leah.

LEAH. You've lost like ten pounds.

GEORGIE. Every cloud.

> *Beat.*

> What do you want?

LEAH. You looking forward to going home?

GEORGIE. Not particularly. God knows what state I left it in.

LEAH. I tidied.

GEORGIE. What?

LEAH. I've been feeding Boris Johnson, haven't I?

GEORGIE. Oh Jesus. I forgot. Is he okay?

LEAH. He's fine. He's fat. You're not very house-proud are you? Not like my mum.

GEORGIE. Yeah well.

LEAH. It's cool though. I cleaned it up. But I think you might have pissed somewhere. Boris Johnson kept sniffing it.

GEORGIE. Oh God.

LEAH. I gave it a sponge down and a squirt of Febreze.

GEORGIE. I haven't got any Febreze.

LEAH. I took some round.

GEORGIE. Please, Leah, don't tell your mum.

LEAH. What's it worth?

GEORGIE. What? Oh, Leah, not this *again*! I can't stay here with you while they go to Kefalonia. I can't be responsible for you, I'm not fit to be. And your mum would never let me.

LEAH. It's not that.

GEORGIE. Good.

LEAH. And I asked that when I thought spending a week with you would be fun. Didn't realise you were going to sleep and cry for an entire month.

GEORGIE. Sorry I haven't been more entertaining.

LEAH. Whatever.

Beat.

GEORGIE. What is it you want then?

LEAH. Can you be honest with me, Auntie Georgie?

GEORGIE. What about?

LEAH. What happened to you?

Beat.

GEORGIE. Look, Leah, I really don't want to get into this.

LEAH. Why does everyone treat me like a child?

GEORGIE. I'm sorry. It's personal –

LEAH. You've been staying in my bed for *four weeks*! I've had to sleep on the sofa and feed your spastic cat every day. Don't you think I deserve the truth? No one in this family tells me anything.

GEORGIE. Look I don't know what happened. Okay? I went out, got drunk, okay, got *more* than drunk... probably. Behaved like a prick. Made a fool of myself. Can't remember.

LEAH. Bullshit.

GEORGIE. It's not bullshit, Leah.

LEAH. But what about all your injuries?

GEORGIE. I probably just… fell over a bit.

LEAH. Yeah right. (*Beat.*) Bet you told Mum what happened.

GEORGIE. *No* I *didn't*!

LEAH. What so no one knows?

GEORGIE. No.

Beat.

LEAH. Did you have a nervous breakdown?

GEORGIE. Maybe. Yes. Probably.

LEAH. Sophie's mum had a nervous breakdown when her husband left her.

GEORGIE. Right.

LEAH. She went nuts in a shop.

GEORGIE. Did she?

LEAH. Yeah. Didn't take her clothes off though.

Beat. Too far? Then they laugh together. Laughter fades. GEORGIE hands LEAH back her pyjamas neatly folded.

GEORGIE. Here.

LEAH. Keep them. I'm not a fan of, sharing… You know.

GEORGIE. I'll give you some money.

LEAH. They're only Primarni.

GEORGIE (*smiles*). Thanks.

LEAH. Was it because of Jamie?

Beat.

GEORGIE. Maybe.

LEAH. I liked him.

GEORGIE. Yeah. Everyone liked him.

LEAH. He was so lovely.

GEORGIE. Yep.

LEAH. And so fit.

GEORGIE. Yeah. (*Beat*.) What? Was he?

LEAH. Hell yeah!

GEORGIE. Oh. Yeah. Well, I suppose he was.

LEAH. So why did you split?

GEORGIE. I don't think you'd understand.

LEAH. Try me!

    Beat. GEORGIE *thinks*.

GEORGIE. I was too much for him. I… exhausted him.

LEAH (*nonplussed*). What does that mean?

GEORGIE. Nothing. I think he wanted to have a baby.

LEAH. Well, why didn't you?

GEORGIE. Come on, Leah. Can you really see me as a mother?

LEAH. Why not?

GEORGIE. I can barely look after myself.

LEAH. You'd be okay.

    Beat. *Quite a compliment for* GEORGIE.

    Mum said it was because of Granddad.

GEORGIE. What?

LEAH. She said it was because you never really grieved for him and Grandma never spoke about him and you had stored up all your sadness and this was it coming out.

GEORGIE. Did she?

    LEAH *nods*.

LEAH. She said my dad helped her come to terms with it – and that Jamie had helped you but now he was gone and you were… fucked… basically. Well, she didn't say fucked but you know what I mean.

GEORGIE. Yeah. I know what you mean.

LEAH. Do you think that's what it is?

GEORGIE. Maybe. (*Beat*.) God. It sounds so weird to hear you call him Granddad. My dad. I mean you never knew him.

LEAH. Mum always showed us pictures and made us say his name.

GEORGIE. Really? That's… That's nice.

LEAH. You too.

GEORGIE. What?

LEAH. The whole time you were travelling, in Nepal and India she used to show us pictures and make us say Auntie Georgina. You looked so exotic. With all your beads. And then when you came home and moved to Kilburn, and you wouldn't see her. She still showed us pictures then.

GEORGIE. Did she?

LEAH. Yeah.

GEORGIE. I had no idea.

LEAH. She's not as icy as you think she is. I mean I always think she's icy, the ice queen I used to call her. But she can be warm.

GEORGIE. She can. I know. If you want icy try Grandma.

Beat.

LEAH. So?

GEORGIE. God! Why is it so important to you?

LEAH. It just is.

GEORGIE. Why?

LEAH. Because I want to know you trust me and that you think of me as an adult.

GEORGIE. *Why?*

LEAH. Because I have something I really need to fucking talk about and I think you're the only person I can talk to and if I don't talk to someone soon I think I'm going to fucking explode!

GEORGIE. Jesus. I'm not sure I am the right person to speak to, Leah. Can't you talk to your mum?

LEAH. No way!

GEORGIE. What about a teacher or a friend at school?

LEAH. No. Auntie Georgie, it has to be you.

GEORGIE *sighs*.

GEORGIE. Okay. Okay.

Beat.

Sometimes people want to hurt themselves, Leah. Destroy themselves. And they find all different ways to do it, drink, drugs, gambling…

LEAH. Sex?

GEORGIE. Maybe. Maybe sex. So anyway, I tried to destroy myself because I was very very unhappy and it nearly worked. I nearly did it. But thanks to your mum and you and Alex and your dad I didn't and now I'm at the beginning of a very long, very dark road but it feels okay to be here. Happy now?

LEAH. I guess.

GEORGIE. What do you need to talk about?

Pause.

LEAH. When did you lose your virginity?

Beat. GEORGIE *is not comfortable talking about this but forces herself as she wants to keep her promise*.

GEORGIE. I was a little bit younger than you. New Year's Eve. 1999.

LEAH. What was it like?

GEORGIE. Quick and cramped. It was in the back of a Ford Fiesta.

LEAH. But did it feel good?

GEORGIE. Good? No, not good… but it was safe. It was with someone I knew and I liked. A bit. He was nice to me. I mean he drove me home afterwards.

LEAH. So he wasn't your boyfriend?

GEORGIE. No he was a friend. I had quite a lot of friends when I was growing up.

LEAH. What about my mum?

GEORGIE. Oh, Leah, I don't think I can get into –

LEAH. Please!

GEORGIE. Okay. I guess she was sixteen maybe.

LEAH. Who was it with?

GEORGIE. Leah!

LEAH. I promise I will *never* tell.

GEORGIE. It was with the lab technician at the school.

LEAH. How old was he?

GEORGIE. I don't know. Twenty-five?

LEAH. Twenty-five? Fuck off!

GEORGIE (*laughing*). It was a bit of a scandal. I think your mum was jealous of all my adventures so she wanted to have one of her own.

LEAH. Get IN, Mum!

GEORGIE. Shhhh! She would fucking KILL ME if she knew I told you that.

LEAH. Do you think she enjoyed it?

Beat.

GEORGIE. I think so, yes.

LEAH. Do you enjoy it?

Pause.

GEORGIE. Sometimes.

Beat.

Do *you* enjoy it?

Pause. LEAH *begins to cry.*

What's the matter, Leah?

Beat.

Leah? What's wrong?

LEAH. I've done something bad.

GEORGIE. Have you?

LEAH. I've done something proper. I can't take it back.

GEORGIE. What is it?

LEAH. And it felt so weird when it was happening but I still let it happen anyway!

GEORGIE. Oh fucking hell, Leah

LEAH. I was drunk… And I feel ashamed.

LEAH *cries.* GEORGIE *tries to hold her.*

GEORGIE. It's okay. We all feel ashamed of things but it won't last. Everything is transient.

LEAH. Not this.

GEORGIE. Yes. Yes it is. Tell me.

LEAH. Oh God oh God! Okay. I let… I let…

GEORGIE. Go on.

LEAH. I LET SOPHIE GO DOWN ON ME.

Pause.

GEORGIE *begins to laugh wildly.*

What? Why are you laughing?

GEORGIE (*composing herself*). Nothing. Nothing, sweetheart.

LEAH. This is fucking serious, Auntie Georgie! I've had oral sex with a girl!

GEORGIE. I know. I know I'm sorry. I just thought you'd been… I thought you'd been…

LEAH. What? Raped?

GEORGIE. Yeah.

LEAH. I told you I let it happen. How can that be rape?

GEORGIE. Yeah. No. You're right. Sorry.

LEAH. I thought you'd understand.

GEORGIE *is strangely touched and intrigued.*

GEORGIE. I do. I do understand. Tell me about it.

LEAH *gets up and crosses to the chair.*

Did it feel nice?

Beat.

LEAH. Yeah. I mean it felt strange and wrong and all of that, but at the same time like, my body felt amazing. Like I thought sex was meant to feel like. Like with Luke I enjoyed the feeling sexy bit, but I didn't enjoy the way sex actually felt. Does that make sense?

GEORGIE. Yeah.

LEAH. I think Sophie must be pretty fucking good at it.

GEORGIE. Right.

LEAH. Not that I've got anything to compare it to.

GEORGIE. Did you…

LEAH. What? Cum? I don't think so. I never have. But I think I felt something that felt like the beginning of what could be… that.

GEORGIE. Well that's – that's good.

LEAH. Do you think I'm gay?

GEORGIE. No. I don't think anything about it.

LEAH. I don't think I want to be gay.

GEORGIE. I don't think it means that, sweetheart.

LEAH. Do you think I'm a slut?

GEORGIE. Fuck no! Come on, Leah, you're having fun. Experimenting.

LEAH. Don't patronise me.

GEORGIE. Sorry. How did it happen?

Beat.

LEAH. You know that guy Luke –

GEORGIE. The one who called up at the window drunk?

LEAH. Yeah. He dumped me, just like that. Then he posted the word 'Vanilla' on my timeline and basically the whole of my year saw it before I took it down. All because I didn't want to do this thing that he wanted me to do. I was in a state so I called Soph. I thought she might say 'I told you so', I've barely seen her for two months and she hated Luke, but she was amazing. She said to come over and we'd get secretly pissed and post shit about his dick on Facebook. So we drank two bottles of her mum's Echo Falls and I started telling her how he came in like thirty seconds and how he would never even go down on me. And she was like 'What?' And I was like 'Yeah'. See Sophie went to music camp this summer and she said an oboe player went down on her and it was fucking amazing. She described it all to me in loads of detail. What it felt like when she came. And it made me feel… Well. She asked if I wanted to try it and I just said yeah. We were in her living room. Her mum was at Legs, Bums and Tums.

GEORGIE. That all sounds very exciting, Leah.

LEAH. She's been my best friend for ever.

GEORGIE. I know. Little Sophie! It seems like only yesterday you were picking blackberries together. Now she's going down on you.

GEORGIE *begins to laugh again*

LEAH. Shut up please! Oh God, this is so weird!

GEORGIE. Life is weird.

Beat

So, what now?

LEAH. I don't know. I'm so confused!

GEORGIE. Would you like to... pursue this thing with Sophie?

LEAH. I don't know. She's been texting. I haven't replied –

GEORGIE. Because it doesn't mean you're gay.

LEAH. Okay.

GEORGIE. And if you were gay – that wouldn't be a problem.

LEAH. I guess so...

GEORGIE. What's important is that you're enjoying yourself, Leah. That you feel comfortable, and relaxed, and – and properly turned on, you know?

LEAH. I think the truth is... Oh God.

GEORGIE. Go on.

LEAH *takes a deep breath*

LEAH. I think I'd like to give the whole thing a break.

GEORGIE. Right.

LEAH. I mean now I know that it can feel like that. I think I might like to wait. For a year. Or two, even.

GEORGIE. Okay.

LEAH. Does that make me fucking frigid?

GEORGIE. No. No, sweetheart. Not At All.

LEAH. I mean I wouldn't want anyone to know I *wasn't* having sex. But they don't need to know do they?

GEORGIE. Exactly.

LEAH. I am a woman. I know I need to act like a woman but I –

GEORGIE. Leah. You've got all the time in the world.

LEAH. Okay. Thanks, Auntie Georgie. (*Beat*.) I think I might just start calling you Georgie if that's okay.

GEORGIE. Sure.

LEAH (*sighs a sigh of relief*). All the time in the world.

GEORGIE. Yeah. Why rush things?

LEAH. Yeah. (*Beat*.) Unless I meet a fit guy in Kefalonia then I might just let him fuck my brains out on the beach.

GEORGIE. Leah!

LEAH. 'Black out with my rack out.'

GEORGIE. What?

LEAH. Nothing. I'm joking! (*Beat*.) Probably.

GEORGIE (*unsure*). Okay.

Pause. Suddenly GEORGIE *is filled with an impulse to share some advice with her.*

Leah.

LEAH. What?

Long pause. GEORGIE *cannot find the words.*

GEORGIE. Nothing. Thank you for letting me stay in your room.

GEORGIE *gets up and puts the pyjamas in her holdall. Beat.*

LEAH. Do you think I'm going to be alright?

GEORGIE. Yeah. Yeah, I do.

GEORGIE *zips up the holdall and looks around the room to see if she has left anything. She puts it on her shoulder. She goes to leave.*

Lights fade.

End.

Other Titles in this Series

A Nick Hern Book

Freak first published in Great Britain in 2014 as a paperback original by Nick Hern Books Limited, The Glasshouse, 49a Goldhawk Road, London W12 8QP in association with Theatre503, London and Polly Ingham Productions

Freak copyright © 2014 Anna Jordan

Anna Jordan has asserted her moral right to be identified as the author of this work

Cover image: Emily Tull (www.emilytull.co.uk), designed by Martyn Wainwright

Designed and typeset by Nick Hern Books, London
Printed in Great Britain by Mimeo Ltd, Huntingdon, Cambridgeshire PE29 6XX

A CIP catalogue record for this book is available from the British Library

ISBN 978 1 84842 427 2